i am this girl

i am this girl

gina marie bernard

HEADMISTRESS PRESS

ISBN 978-0-9995930-9-7

Cover art by Hannah Hoch, *Platonische Liebe* (Platonic Love) (1930). Public Domain. Cover & book design by Mary Meriam.

PUBLISHER
Headmistress Press
60 Shipview Lane
Sequim, WA 98382
Telephone: 917-428-8312
Email: headmistresspress@gmail.com
Website: headmistresspress.blogspot.com

dedicated to anyone who has ever struggled with identity—
may you come to know your strength, trust your beauty,
and be at peace with your truth

contents

i am this girl

who conceived a second language,
composed hollow expletives—
the exequies of failed intention;

dreamed of replacing herself,
taking herself from behind—glass
cracked, face ground against mirrors;

swallowed prescriptions, areolas aching—
azaleas blossoming against
the heartbreak of corrosion;

fists fixed & lashing out—
teeth bared in naked rancor;
her carriage scarred, carnage

unleashed in fractured anger—
halved but somehow still whole;
who flowered like earnest ashes

from burn barrel desire.

Wraiths

A finch fluttered about the kitchen,
and as I cupped her between palms
she quivered, a heart in arrhythmia;

my bathroom mirror shattered against tile
at two a.m., shards as brilliant in moon burn
as the wings of a million nightmare moths;

I placed an acorn in my window sill,
but the pane was already fissured like sky
under a vast and approaching storm;

shadows haunt the verge of my lawn,
and deep into the night I hear frogs calling
to other frogs—the mimicry of owls.

Decisions float on beds of glacial regret;
And at my back, blue hills rise like mist upon
themselves. I step from these convulsions

and cold, green water arrests my breath.
But I'm suddenly knee deep and thirsty,
striding through the surf.

Dry Drowning

The farmer tilts his Monsanto cap back from the bronze horizon of his forehead, stabs a finger to Formica with enough force to rattle silverware, and swears to God—and those of us in the café—that he most assuredly has found a writhing bowfin buried in the black soil of his north forty some weeks after April's flood has drained from this lower field.

. . .

Tonight, dreams fan alluvial—I inhale lithified sediment, chambers fat with artifact:

a hailstorm of fisted stone,
flint arrowheads,
Prince Albert tobacco tins,
spent shotgun shells,
pull-tab Schlitz cans,
a cracked telephone insulator,
the cobalt-stepped sundown,
antlers, branched and broken.

To breathe this tannin-stained leaf litter—
an arboretum sewn into my tongue.

The deluge recedes.
I drift back to surface consciousness.
Staring through the fallow dark,
the images now dormant—

I entomb myself deep in blankets, trying to recall the last time we made love.

Susan

grant me strength to cede you,

to enunciate strictures of clubbed apology
long lodged within my heart.

my spine pulp; jawbone heavy,
shedding mossed teeth into carpets
of mushrooming grief.

a reservoir spread over my banks
sable as any raven's breast—

this levy delinquent years before we met.

how many pounds of flesh did i excise
before ripping along the suture we'd stitched

together?

something in me metastasized—fed
this pleurisy; resuscitates pain.

stooped and coughing awful blood,
i now grovel through combs of faithless rain—

forever seeking you in metaphor.

ordering off the menu

the onset of another panic attack settles
as i contemplate lunch at Zorbaz,
a restaurant chain whose towering menu
boasts world-class pizza and Mexican.

exhuming the contents of my purse,
i fail to unearth any Ativan—anxiety pressed
like funeral loam beneath my trembling nails.

when have my friends begun mouthing
soundless dialogue—actresses awaiting
voice-over in a colossal lizard film?

an alien impersonating our waitress
wends nearer, leering;

customers,
ornately painted marionettes, dance
on monofilament,

and when it is my turn to order

i say i would like

to prick myself with a safety pin
and curl about the ceiling, the inside of my deflating skin
turned out, still moist from my final exhalation.

i would like

to press fingers through my eyes;
to pluck them from my skull;
to wear them like puppet olives, pimentos
streaming from the rootless hollows.

i need

my fucking brain washed
in bucketed bleach solution—left overnight
to soak clean these petitions
stained with so much fierce peril.

pardon me

these tics and guttural explosives,
the elocutions of a braying hyena.

may i please

shed my clothes across the parking lot,
cocoon myself in penitent wool,
swallow this tongue swollen with detestation,
French inhale exhaust from a length of garden hose?

and did i mention *i need all of this to go!*

Secrets

: i :

mound in spaded basement earth, its cool breath unspooling worm silk about your ankles;

: ii :

school like whiskered catfish rising blindly through silted current to gulp burnished air, mouths lipped like open ulcers;

: iii :

whisper with Leonard Cohen through the hiss of a lost station as your brake lights blink feline down another back alley;

: iv :

witness the consumptive specter haunting your desktop monitor;

: v :

surge in spasms of searing shame that roil like serpents into bowls of morning porcelain;

: vi :

swarm like ants to the seed you once spilled amid a green haze of ordered corn, your father's stolen *Playboy* again interred inside a rusting Folger's can;

: vii :

lie beneath the stage-paint smile you've smeared from ear to year.

: viii :

But time unveils how you've spent your life—capering down tilted hallways to punch fists through these funhouse mirrors.

Unsettled

Railway steel sings,
pending winter freight.

Buntings startle a washwater sky.

March hares draft hesitant
script upon this daybreak.

Our house stirs keen,
evening's fight cut short.

Window view—the cat's eraser nose
spots cloudy glass.

With skeletal lilacs
I compose cursive blows.

She descends without a word.

My lips part, the outline
of a battening moon.

Heading West, Across Montana

Empty highway fashions drowsy music—
yellow notes singing sleep as they speed past.
Here, sky yawns blue all afternoon. Telephone lines

keep time—rise high, swing low in waves that tie horizons.
I squint, sun fierce in my eyes, sure for a moment
her face, or its brief outline, peers windswept

from the rushing grass. Miles now swell between
pockets of thought as shimmering as lost oases.
Exhausted, a raging sun gives up another day

to undulating darkness. Somewhere under this night
of sage and purple rock, she lies down. Tomorrow, dawn
will find her in easy slumber—sheets cool about her body

like green and climbing land. So I drive toward distant buttes,
my longing an endless, empty interstate that ribbons west
to meet her dreams.

Vixen

The fox appears beneath
a meridian sun. She circles
the coop unaware of her cliché,
or that I've recently employed
the hatchet wedged into the soft
face of the killing block.
She's fluid movement,
a flush brushstroke across
the canvas of my backyard.
I've seen her before: stealthily
hunting mice in tall summer grass,
or poised mid-air, a bass clef
above sheets of midnight snow.
Each time it is like tending
to fractions of myself—promiscuity,
pursuant, corsair. I long to attest
to her life of singular appetite.
But in the next moment
she has gone, leaving nothing
but a hushed draft striking
tones upon my pilfered heart.

tributaries

at first,	dread thundered—lightning stalking a rainless sky;
at fault,	i plied her with shallow guile
at a loss	to express depth of self.
at any rate,	which words would accord my carried load?
at last	i grasped my chance had swept downstream
beyond	the point.
by mistake	she plunged in the obscure pool where
by myself	i'd kept legs churning, chin tipped against drowning.
by rote	i respired an effluence of exercised lies, revived
by the way	she breathed for us both, and
for a while	our plot was not flooded.
in any case,	i mouthed more bedded mud, channeled destruction
in vain	attempt to arrest an image i'd been banking—
in itself	a levee already breached by the surge,
in danger	always of eroding at our conflux.
in the end,	i struck a match to poured oil, and set our marriage
on fire.	refusing to ford this burning river, she turned from my flames.
under no	illusion she'll return, my body now floats just
underneath	the surface: fish have eaten my eyes, and skin drifts like cotton
with the	current from these bones delta-bound.

Proof

you lie beside me, lithe curves bathed in aurulent light.
dawn arrives—soft as your sleeping breath.

i dream you stand barelegged before the board; i watch
you push back the sleeves of my oversized shirt.

"i mill my own wheat," you say. the flour in your hair—
that dusts your wrists—makes my desire leaven.

"it's better if i cut the fat," you advise. knives and butter
and sugar crumble until you are not there.

a comforter enfolds you like kneaded dough.
i hear the kitchen timer, the grating of an oven door.

i rise to one elbow, the balm of yeast pregnant.
reaching to punch it down,

i wake alone to a gnawing hunger.

frequency

straining, i can just brush the face of her Crosley AM radio.
this artifact—circa 1932—has cathedral sides that arch
together like hands held in prayer. beneath this veneered relic,
lips kiss hips, spread labia, seek clitoris in fevered avidity.

the dial rests between stations, ghostly voices vying with her
passionate pleas for my attention.

first a Mexican bullfight:

the matador poised and glittering in his *traje de luces,*
cape drawn across horn—the final caesura in this dance.
my tongue, a *banderilla,* darts beneath her pink hood.

below the static comes an ethereal reading—public radio
from somewhere far outside the *corrida de toros.* in flat
Midwestern tones, the host reads from the collected works
of Angelina Weld Grimké.

moonlight bathes the studio as i discover her body in silent
plagiarism, my breath a soft wind upon her glistening skin.

much later, she sighs and asks—a drowsy lover's murmur—

if i will turn the radio down. i reach up ready to comply
but pause when i hear the deep rhythm of her sudden sleep.
in the dark i close my eyes and listen. the frequencies
have died away. white noise returns me to her bed—

this hallowed midnight chancel.

Nigromancy

Dysphoria is a campaigning sorceress; / a Svengali that conjures itself, / learns rote a duplicitous augury, / and cuts each deck false; / a fakir scrawling across papyrus / mystic avatars of the severest tortures / and self-mortifications. // Nimbly, I practice sleight of hand / combing cobbled streets for those / to deceive in sating my compulsion. // I riffle through tattered cards, manipulating— / behind each smile / a force that belies free will, / like this inability to sever myself / in half and divorce the shadows / clambering tarpaulin walls. // Often now misdirection collapses, / the matrix fails, my rings unlink, / and manic patter cannot draw attention / from the sickly sheen of flop sweat / glistening my brow. // Horrified, I pinch shut eyes. // Fingers pressed to temples, I summon myself / as you enter this parlor. // A brace of startled doves unfurls / about us like a silver parasol. // Despite fervent cries, I cannot escape / my long-destined malediction / and disappear in choking tendrils / vaporized before your astonished gaze.

Michelle

bare memory recalled, sharp report, brittle bones exploding—
copper tang like coins upon my tongue.

tonight is austere: words frozen, lips stretched opaque.
this strained landscape, bloodless and blue

as winter horizon, finally cracks—razor-thin fissures
brilliant with keen need. we come together again:

animus yielding to defenseless love. you clutch my hair
in hard fists. my heart catches as i swallow sudden shards

of fucking gravel.

Anatomy

She ponders.

When she still had a penis,
she acted like a prick;

since she got her vagina,
she's often called a cunt.

Is it possible
she's just always been

an asshole?

reading bones

i am sea-mad Ahab pounding this hand with my own ivory stump—
phalanges piercing skin like spy-hopping white whales;

i am the flued harpoon buried deep between shoulder blades; pliers
pulling coined hope from maul-hammered mast;

my hesitation, a drogue in blue currents; insides coiled like dried rope
stowed in salt-crusted barrels;

i am gull-harried slabs of rendering fat, flensed from flesh & set to boil;
lips erupting—cracked heel sunk in slick decks thick with black blood;

first mate to myself, transfixed in duty—condemned by craven obligation;
i'm coffined carpenter, orphaned child, & the third day's dark shadow;

i tongue prophecies at a copper sun, still surprised at my blindness—
my death stirring in the trigonometry of stars.

to feel small / is no great chore

simply crawl on your belly / through overgrown grass / your breasts pressed to an earth / surreptitiously laced / silent spinnerets ensnaring / incalculable numbers

to feel diseased / is easy enough

just as effortless as reciting symptoms / while shivering in drenched sheets / feverishly repeating contagions / to the warren of dust bunnies / under your bed

to feel corrupt / is a matter of course

merely gulp despair like curdled milk / cramp / collapse to the floor / your disgrace pouring down / the backs of your legs

to feel deformed / demands little more

than peering in mirrors / marveling at surgical scars / convinced your feminized face / costumes the contours / of a disfigured heart

to feel broken / becomes normal

a scratched record of echoes / filtering from voided hallways / always empty / like you

this pain then / proves palpable

like the sting of fine fangs / fastened to your spine / the septic bite of some / repulsive spider

Anagrams

I happen upon this generator
while trailing bread crumbs
deep into the vast wilderness
of online ennui. Dubious at first,

I enter my name: *Gina Marie Bernard.*
Instantly, a wake of portent sluices
down my screen. Deeply affected,
I cannot shake the prescient results:

marinara being red is too obvious;
bare maid earn grin, while improper—
both politically and grammatically—
positively makes me smile.

I've never been to an *area barring denim,*
or read of an *Indiana bra merger,*
but they are no more atypical than
a hostler's *rare mane braiding* technique.

Not that I concur with everything.

There is, after all, something sordid
about *Anna Reamer Brigid* and
Armenian Bag Rider—like DVDs
shelved behind seedy curtains.

Equally vulgar is the marriage
of the *Arian German bride*
to her *Arab-arming denier.*

Later, I awake from a vision
wherein I've been served
upon buttered crackers
paired with a costly wine
at the *Anagram Brie Diner.*

Consider the irony—a nightmare
of Beaujolais, stone wheat,
margarine, and brie!

Grappling this dreadful dream—
brain drain meager—I see signs
everywhere:

bad inner marriage.
(I am divorced.)

Rabid anger remain.
(I repeat, I am divorced!)

Bare drag earn mini.
(But at what price? Poor queen!)

Air bed near margin!
(Too ominous to ponder.)

But like any brave *gabardine mariner,*
I will weather this bitter storm
in tightly woven garments—
the *remainder bargain* a mantra
to ward off anathema:
drama rare in being, drama rare in being...

But I have been infected,
anagrams burning all around me.
The charred remnants rise,
not like a *game bird near rain,*
but instead like wrathful crows,

and they've eaten all my bread crumbs.

Corpus delicti

Autopsy Report: BPD699308-18J

DECEDENT: ~~First Middle~~ (dead name!) ~~Last~~

Autopsy authorized (enthusiastically!) by: You, the Self-Righteous
Identified by: fingers stabbing & attendant rafts of spastic laughter

Rigor: the unyielding immodesty to live her own truth
Livor: purpled abhorrence—lungs burst, breath expelled against your mammoth enmity
Distribution: she was your daughter—denial condemns you!
Age: she grew up—try doing the same!
Sex: your hurtful pronouns—he/she & it; that *thing* you all called a petri-dish experiment
Length: a life sentence with no possibility of parole
Weight: a community's intolerance garroting her neck
Eyes: bore witness to your ballistic bigotry
Hair: uprooted in fistfuls of clutched delirium
Body Heat: her immersion-burned brain scorched with concentric charring

CLOTHING:

1. Bra and panties—that's what matters, right? Her identity reduced to made-for-television pasquinades of flashbulb farce: abraded waist, cross-dressing lace stuffed past lipstick-smeared teeth.

2. Merino wool sweater—but you were the wolves snapping at tendons; a pack gorging torn flesh before she expired.

X-RAYS: reveal her agency fractured by the compounding force of blunt trauma.

HISTORY: His story. *His.* You never let her forget that.

PATHOLOGICAL DIAGNOSES: Forty-nine years of self interrogation with no probable cause.

GROSS DESCRIPTION: Indeed! Acid scalding your throats—bile rising to blister compassion.

SUMMARY: Leviticus 20:13! Her life was a blood-cursed abomination; her death, your God's command.

CAUSE OF DEATH: "Murica, you fucking faggot!"

MANNER OF DEATH: Manslaughter. *Man* Slaughter. Slaughter. Laughter. Her.

picking scabs

like skidding out
across black tar—

Huffy scuffed
naked ankle
loose shoe lost

gray morning
hid in bed
itching lingers

fingers worry
dried apricot
flick at it

pizza crust
wells of blood
bubble up

sweet release
spinal twinge
once again

but somehow
always in my brain

things at which i excel

equating my inability to print a plausible farewell
with an amassed lack of passable pride;

sweeping away traces of eraser—palmed graphite
already smudging left handed paper;

leaving this morning's poured coffee to cool
like any commitment i've desperately courted;

recycling the same five dishes to drip from my rack,
hard water rusting white sink a bit darker;

monitoring pulse threads as i pause at end caps
to avoid forcing friends into aisled conversation;

failing to forgive my father or to have faith in myself—
always asking instead if i'm indeed even worthy;

justifying my addiction for what has obviously passed—
bygone scripts in which i prefer to play victim;

listening to eared whispers intimating i have not earned love—
a tortured son brought into the world, undeserving;

bleeding now as a daughter, still lost in storms of thought
revolving undone in ever smaller spaces.

Acknowledgments

Many thanks to the editors of the following publications, in which these poems appeared, sometimes in earlier versions:

Bone & Ink: "Nigromancy"

Fox Cry Review: "Vixen"

Heavy Feather Review: "Wraiths," "Dry Drowning," "Susan"

Ink & Voices: "Anatomy," "tributaries"

Meat for Tea: "Anagrams"

Prism: "Heading West, Across Montana"

Skin to Skin: The Art of the Lesbian: "Proof," "frequency"

Spider Mirror: "ordering off the menu," "Secrets," "Unsettled"

S/tick: "Michelle"

Susan / The Journal: "things at which i excel"

Utterance Journal: "picking scabs," "reading bones," "to feel small"

About the Author

gina marie bernard is a heavily tattooed transgender woman, retired roller derby vixen, and full-time English teacher. She holds B.A., B.S., and M.A. degrees from Bemidji State University. Her daughters, Maddie and Parker, own her heart. She is the author of the young adult novel *Alpha Summer* (Loonfeather Press, 2005) and the chapbook *Naked, Getting Nuder* (Clare Songbirds Publications, 2018). She can be reached at her website: ginamariebernard.squarespace.com

Headmistress Press Books

She/Her/Hers - Amy Lauren

Spoiled Meat - Nicole Santalucia

Cake - Jen Rouse

The Salt and the Song - Virginia Petrucci

mad girl's crush tweet - summer jade leavitt

Saturn coming out of its Retrograde - Briana Roldan

i am this girl - gina marie bernard

Week/End - Sarah Duncan

My Girl's Green Jacket - Mary Meriam

Nuts in Nutland - Mary Meriam, Hannah Barrett

Lovely - Lesléa Newman

Teeth & Teeth - Robin Reagler

How Distant the City - Freesia McKee

Shopgirls - Marissa Higgins

Riddle - Diane Fortney

When She Woke She Was an Open Field - Hilary Brown

God With Us - Amy Lauren

A Crown of Violets - Renée Vivien tr. Samantha Pious

Fireworks in the Graveyard - Joy Ladin

Social Dance - Carolyn Boll

The Force of Gratitude - Janice Gould

Spine - Sarah Caulfield

Diatribe from the Library - Farrell Greenwald Brenner

Blind Girl Grunt - Constance Merritt

Acid and Tender - Jen Rouse

Beautiful Machinery - Wendy DeGroat

Odd Mercy - Gail Thomas

The Great Scissor Hunt - Jessica K. Hylton

www.ingramcontent.com/pod-product-compliance
Lightning Source LLC
Chambersburg PA
CBHW072056040426
42447CB00012BB/3144